Irish Wolfhounds

GREAT BIG DOGS

By Kristen Rajczak

Gareth Stevens
Publishing

Please visit our website, www.garethstevens.com. For a free color catalog of all our high-quality books, call toll free 1-800-542-2595 or fax 1-877-542-2596.

Library of Congress Cataloging-in-Publication Data

Rajczak, Kristen.
Irish wolfhounds / Kristen Rajczak.
    p. cm. — (Great big dogs)
Includes index.
ISBN 978-1-4339-5780-2 (pbk.)
ISBN 978-1-4339-5781-9 (6-pack)
ISBN 978-1-4339-5778-9 (library binding)
1. Irish wolfhound—Juvenile literature. I. Title.
SF429.I85R35 2011
636.753'5—dc22

                                    2010046049

First Edition

Published in 2012 by
Gareth Stevens Publishing
111 East 14th Street, Suite 349
New York, NY 10003

Copyright © 2012 Gareth Stevens Publishing

Designer: Andrea Davison-Bartolotta
Editor: Kristen Rajczak

Photo credits: Cover, pp. 1, 6, 13, 18, 20 Shutterstock.com; p. 5 Carl Lyttle/Stone/Getty Images; p. 9 Gerard Brown/Dorling Kindersley/Getty Images; p. 10 Brian Arch/WireImage/Getty Images; p. 14 Scott Barbour/Getty Images; p. 17 Carl De Souza/AFP/Getty Images.

Printed in the United States of America

CPSIA compliance information: Batch #CS11GS: For further information contact Gareth Stevens, New York, New York at 1-800-542-2595.

Contents

Words in the glossary appear in **bold** type the first time they are used in the text.

Giant Breed

Irish wolfhounds are one of the tallest **breeds** of dog. They usually grow to about 30 to 35 inches (76 to 89 cm) tall at the shoulder. However, they can also be much taller! Irish wolfhounds are not very heavy for their height. They weigh about 105 to 120 pounds (48 to 54 kg).

For centuries, Irish wolfhounds were used to hunt and guard property. They fought in wars. Today, they're most commonly kept as pets.

Fully grown Irish wolfhounds stand taller than many other breeds.

Irish wolfhounds'
coats can be many
different colors.

Long and Lean

Irish wolfhounds have a lean body and a long neck and head. When they stand on their back legs, some are 7 feet (2.1 m) tall! They have deep chests and large frames. Their coats are not smooth. Irish wolfhounds have a **rough** outer coat and a soft inner coat. They may be gray, **brindle**, red, black, white, or **fawn**. Most Irish wolfhound owners don't clip their dog's fur. As a result, Irish wolfhounds have a natural, hairy look.

Sight Hounds

Irish wolfhounds are sight hounds. Sight hounds, or gazehounds, hunt by using sight rather than their sense of smell. Sight hounds can see **prey** from far away. They're fast runners. Sight hounds need to be fenced in to stop them from chasing things they see in the distance.

Many sight hounds race other dogs in an event called **lure** coursing. The dogs chase a fake rabbit. They're judged on how fast they run, how well they follow the lure, and if they seem to enjoy it.

Dog Tales

Greyhounds and whippets are other sight hound breeds.

This Irish wolfhound's long legs and light frame help it move quickly.

9

Dog Tales

Irish wolfhounds were named for their main prey—wolves.

Irish wolfhounds do not fight today, but they are honored by the Army National Guard. ▷

10

Hound History

Irish wolfhounds are one of the oldest dog breeds. Records of these dogs date back more than 2,000 years! In Ireland, the Irish wolfhound was used to hunt wolves, elk, and wild pigs. They were such good hunters that wolves became **extinct** in Ireland. Irish wolfhounds also fought in wars. Their size and speed made them good helpers for soldiers. They pulled men off horses and stood guard.

Royal Companions

In ancient Ireland, the Irish wolfhound was a sign of wealth. Only nobles owned them. It was common for Irish wolfhounds to be given as gifts. They were usually given to kings and other royalty. The breed spread all over the world. However, so many Irish wolfhounds left Ireland this way that the breed almost disappeared from Ireland in the early 1800s. There was also less need for the dogs in Ireland because there was very little prey left for them to hunt.

Dog Tales
In 1652, it became illegal for Irish wolfhounds to leave Ireland.

Today, Irish wolfhounds are still wonderful companions.

13

Dog Tales

Captain George Augustus Graham, who created modern Irish wolfhounds, served with the East India Company during India's First War of Independence in 1857.

This Irish wolfhound is being judged in a dog show. ▷

Almost Extinct

In the 1800s, Captain George Augustus Graham saved the Irish wolfhound breed. He wanted to bring back the grand dog of the past. The few Irish wolfhounds left in Ireland were small and in poor health. Graham bred dogs like **mastiffs** and deerhounds with Irish wolfhounds to make the breed bigger and stronger.

It worked. The Irish Kennel Club allowed Irish wolfhounds to appear in dog shows beginning in 1879. The American Kennel Club officially recognized the breed in 1897.

Fun with Family

Irish wolfhounds are no longer fearless hunters. Today, they most often live with families. Irish wolfhounds are **loyal** and loving pets. An Irish wolfhound's favorite place to be is with its owner. They're not good guard dogs, even though they're large. They welcome everyone as a friend.

Irish wolfhounds learn quickly. They can be trained to obey. Their calm nature makes them a good fit for families with small children.

Dog Tales

Irish wolfhounds try to fit into your daily life. If you're a coach potato, your Irish wolfhound will be, too!

Irish wolfhounds want to be close to those they love.

17

Dog Tales

Irish wolfhounds should not start training until they are 18 months to 2 years old, when they are fully grown. This helps puppies stay healthy.

This Irish wolfhound puppy will grow much bigger as it gets older!

Staying Healthy

Irish wolfhounds are one of several "giant breeds." Owners of giant-breed dogs know they need special care.

Irish wolfhounds only live about 6 to 8 years. These dogs are so big they often have problems with their heart and bones. Young Irish wolfhounds get hurt easily if they exercise too much. Their bones and joints are still soft and growing. However, Irish wolfhounds should play and have a daily walk to stay healthy.

Owning an Irish Wolfhound

Irish wolfhounds' needs are as big as they are. They need a lot of space to move around—and that might include a bigger family car! These dogs need to stretch their long legs. Irish wolfhounds' food may cost a lot because they eat so much of it. Still, as a family pet, these gentle giants will pay you back with lots of love!

Learning About Irish Wolfhounds

height	30 to 35 inches (76 to 89 cm) at the shoulder
weight	about 105 to 120 pounds (48 to 54 kg)
coloring	gray, brindle, red, black, white, or fawn
life span	6 to 8 years

Glossary

breed: a group of animals that share features different from other groups of the kind

brindle: uneven dark bands on lighter-colored fur

extinct: no longer existing

fawn: a light grayish brown

loyal: faithful

lure: bait

mastiff: a large, powerful dog that has a smooth coat

prey: an animal hunted or killed by another animal for food

rough: not soft

Books

Hart, Joyce. *Big Dogs*. New York, NY: Marshall Cavendish Benchmark, 2008.

Landau, Elaine. *Irish Wolfhounds Are the Best!* Minneapolis, MN: Lerner Publications, 2011.

Websites

Irish Wolfhound
bigdogshugepaws.com/Irish_Wolfhound
Learn more about the breed and a group that helps large dogs.

Irish Wolfhound Club of America
www.iwclubofamerica.org
Find out if an Irish wolfhound is right for you. Learn about training your dog for lure coursing.

Index